THE WORLD'S TOP TENS

THE WORLD'S FASTEST CARS

by **Michael Martin**

Consultant:
Drew Phillips
Site Editor and Coordinator
www.Fast-Autos.net

Capstone
press

Mankato, Minnesota

Edge Books are published by Capstone Press,
151 Good Counsel Drive, P.O. Box 669, Mankato, Minnesota 56002.
www.capstonepress.com

Library of Congress Cataloging-in-Publication Data
Martin, Michael, 1948–
    The world's fastest cars / by Michael Martin.
       p. cm.—(Edge books. The world's top tens)
    Summary: "Describes in countdown format 10 of the world's fastest cars"—Provided
by publisher.
    Includes bibliographical references and index.
    ISBN-13: 978-0-7368-5455-9 (hardcover)
    ISBN-10: 0-7368-5455-X (hardcover)
    1. Automobiles, Racing—Juvenile literature. I. Title. II. World's top ten
(Mankato, Minn.)
TL236.M35255 2006
629.228—dc22   2005019427

Editorial Credits

Angie Kaelberer, editor; Kate Opseth, set designer; Jenny Bergstrom, book designer;
    Kelly Garvin, photo researcher/photo editor

Photo Credits

Bugatti Automobiles, 16, 17, 27 (top right)
Drew Phillips, 18, 27 (middle left)
Getty Images/AFP, cover
Koenigsegg Automotive AB, 12, 26 (bottom right)
Louise Ann Noeth, 4, 14, 20, 21, 22, 24, 25, 27 (top left, middle right,
    bottom left, and bottom right), 29
McLaren.com, 10, 11, 26 (bottom left)
Ron Kimball Stock/Ron Kimball, 6, 8, 9, 26 (top left and top right)

1 2 3 4 5 6 11 10 09 08 07 06

TABLE OF CONTENTS

FAST CARS

The Dodge Viper is the fastest production car made by a U.S. company. But even this sleek machine isn't fast enough to make our top 10 list.

Vroom! What was that streak of silver?

Over the years, drivers have set thousands of different kinds of speed records. That's why making any list of fast cars is tough. A few production cars from factories are designed to be as fast as race cars. These supercars can be driven on ordinary roads. People have also built one-of-a-kind cars designed only to set speed records.

Some car lovers might put different cars on their top 10 lists. Still, one thing is for certain. People who dream of going fast would love to sit behind the wheel of any car on this list.

And if you see one of these cars tearing down the highway, don't blink. You just might miss it.

10

The Murciélago's doors swing forward and up when open.

MURCIÉLAGO

In Spain, people tell a story about a bull named Murciélago. Murciélago still fought after being stabbed 24 times by a bullfighter. Because of the bull's bravery, the bullfighter spared its life. The Italian car company Lamborghini named one of its fastest cars after this tough bull. The car has a top speed of 205 miles (330 kilometers) per hour.

The Murciélago's doors do not swing out when they are opened. Instead, they slide forward and upward. In that position, they look like seagull wings. The gull-wing doors are just one feature that makes this car different from others.

In 2005, Lamborghini began making Murciélagos with convertible tops. The company warned buyers not to drive faster than 100 miles (161 kilometers) per hour with the top up. At high speeds, wind could easily rip off the top.

FIRST MODEL: 2001

HORSEPOWER: 571

TOP SPEED: 205 miles (330 kilometers) per hour

COST: $320,000

9 ENZO FERRARI

The Enzo's engine is in an unusual place. It's in a compartment behind the driver. Many race car engines are also in that spot. The driver has an easier time controlling the car at high speeds with the engine in the middle of the car.

The Enzo is only 45 inches (114 centimeters) high.

The Enzo's engine is behind the driver.

The Enzo's body acts like an upside-down wing. The faster the car goes, the more a downward force pushes it to the road. The car is not far above the road, anyway. It's only 45 inches (114 centimeters) high. Even a 6-year-old would have to bend down to get into an Enzo.

FIRST MODEL:	2002
HORSEPOWER:	660
NUMBER MADE:	399
TOP SPEED:	217 miles (349 kilometers) per hour
COST:	$670,000

8

In 1998, the F1 set a world speed record of 240.1 miles (386.4 kilometers) per hour.

MCLAREN F1

In the early 1990s, McLaren Cars set out to make the fastest production car on the road. The company built 100 McLarens from 1993 to 1998. The rare cars are still worth a lot of money. They can truly be called million-dollar cars.

The F1 held the world speed record for a production car from 1998 until 2005. Not many cars zoom over highways at more than 200 miles (322 kilometers) per hour. Even fewer supercars have room for two passengers to come along for the ride.

The F1's chassis is made of carbon fiber. This material makes the McLaren lightweight, yet strong. It only weighs about 2,800 pounds (1,270 kilograms). That's light for a car that can hold three people.

The F1 has gull-wing doors and a carbon fiber body.

FIRST MODEL: 1993

HORSEPOWER: 627

ENGINE: BMW V-12

TOP SPEED: 240 miles (386 kilometers) per hour

COST: $1,000,000

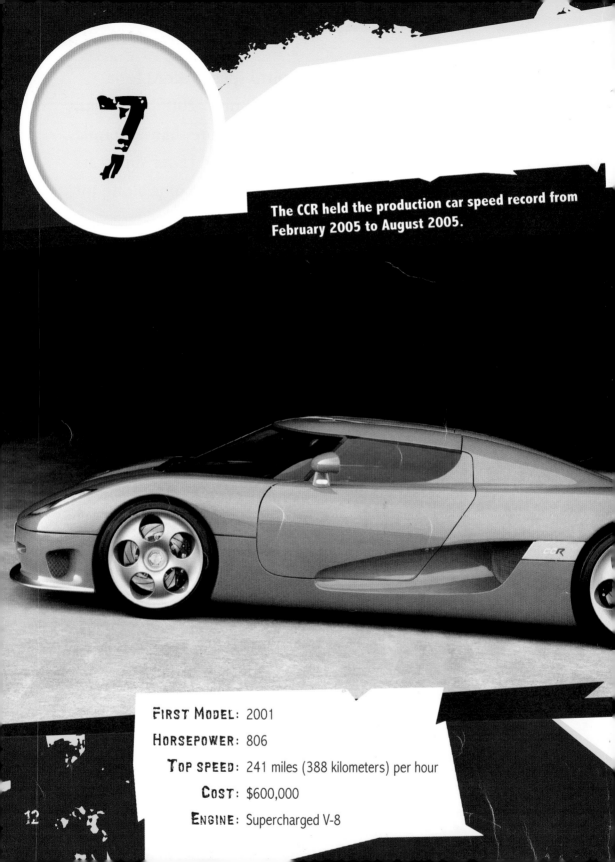

7

The CCR held the production car speed record from February 2005 to August 2005.

FIRST MODEL: 2001

HORSEPOWER: 806

TOP SPEED: 241 miles (388 kilometers) per hour

COST: $600,000

ENGINE: Supercharged V-8

KOENIGSEGG CCR

This Swedish supercar's name might sound funny. But its performance is nothing to laugh about. In February 2005, the Koenigsegg CCR became the fastest production car in the world. It broke the McLaren F1's record by barreling down the road at 241 miles (388 kilometers) per hour. In test runs, the car reached even faster speeds.

To make it more aerodynamic, the car is designed to stay as low to the ground as possible. Some owners add fins to the rear hood. The fins help keep the back end of the car on the road at very high speeds.

The CCR's exhaust system is made out of a shiny metal called titanium. The light, strong metal can stand high temperatures. That's important when handling the exhaust produced by a record-breaking car.

6

White Lightning set its speed record at the Bonneville Salt Flats in Utah.

278

HORSEPOWER: About 400

RECORD SPEED: 246 miles (396 kilometers) per hour

LENGTH: 25 feet (7.6 meters)

WEIGHT: 2,450 pounds (1,111 kilograms)

OWNER: Ed Dempsey

WHITE LIGHTNING

Many people think electric cars have to give up speed to use less fuel. These people have never seen the White Lightning Streamliner.

White Lightning is one of the fastest cars on the planet. In 1999, it set an electric car speed record of 246 miles (396 kilometers) per hour. Since then, it has reached 254 miles (409 kilometers) per hour during test runs.

The car is powered by two electric motors. They get their power from about 6,000 small batteries.

White Lightning is long, narrow, and low to the ground. It is shaped like a pencil. Its shape cuts its wind resistance.

5

The Veyron broke the Koenigsegg CCR's speed record in August 2005.

BUGATTI VEYRON

The Bugatti Veyron looks strong. It should. It is by far the most powerful passenger car ever made. It is also the most expensive. A Bugatti will set you back nearly $1.5 million.

The Veyron's twin-turbo engine produces an amazing 1,001 horsepower. That's even more horsepower than the engine in a NASCAR race car. In only 3 seconds, the Veyron can go from standing still to 60 miles (97 kilometers) per hour. And it reaches 180 miles (290 kilometers) per hour in just 14 seconds.

In August 2005, the Veyron became the fastest production car in the world. It reached an incredible 253 miles (407 kilometers) per hour.

The Bugatti is known for its flashy two-tone paint job.

FIRST MODEL: 2003

HORSEPOWER: 1,001

TOP SPEED: 253 miles (407 kilometers) per hour

ENGINE: W-16 Quad Supercharged

COST: $1,450,000

The Sledgehammer takes just 4 seconds to go from zero to 60 miles (97 kilometers) per hour.

SLEDGEHAMMER

The Sledgehammer might be the fastest car ever built that could also be driven legally on the street. Former racer Reeves Callaway built his own version of the Chevrolet Corvette in 1988.

Only one model was ever made. During speed tests, the Sledgehammer hit 254 miles (409 kilometers) per hour. That's four times the speed limit on most highways.

At 880 horsepower, the Sledgehammer's V-8 engine is one of the most powerful ever. It has two turbochargers that force more air into the engine. The extra air allows the fuel to burn faster and produce tremendous power.

Callaway's engineers offered to make more Sledgehammers at a price of $400,000 each. No one ever took them up on their offer. Maybe drivers were afraid they couldn't handle this powerful machine.

HORSEPOWER: 880

TOP SPEED: 254 miles (409 kilometers) per hour

COST: $400,000

ENGINE: Twin Turbo V-8

BUILDER: Reeves Callaway

3 FLATFIRE

The FlatFire Streamliner looks like a rocket on wheels. But the engine that powers this space-age car comes from a 1946 Ford. It is a flathead engine, which means its valves are in the engine block, instead of in the cylinder head.

The FlatFire set its speed record August 14, 2002, at the Bonneville Salt Flats in Utah.

HORSEPOWER:	700
TOP SPEED:	302 miles (486 kilometers) per hour
ENGINE:	1946 Ford flathead block
OWNER:	Ron Main

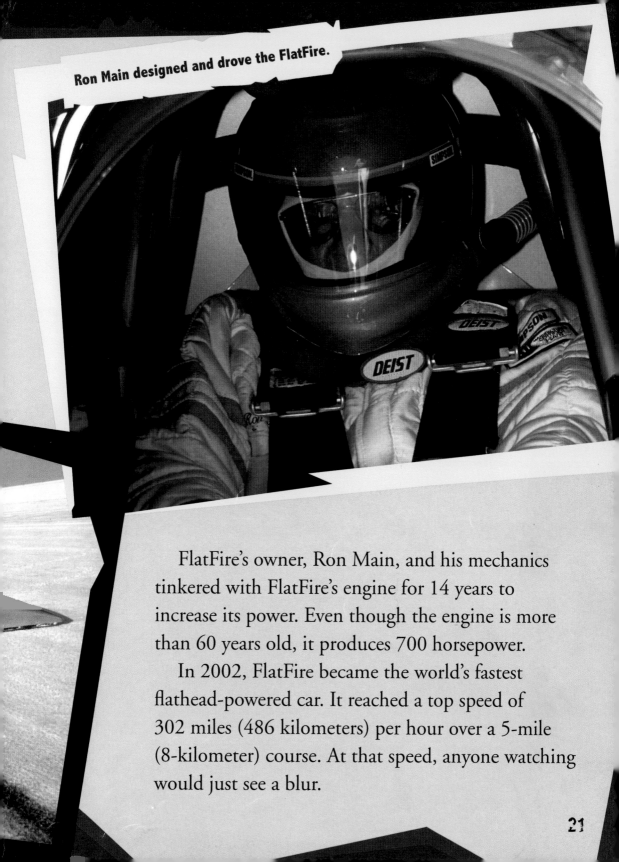

Ron Main designed and drove the FlatFire.

FlatFire's owner, Ron Main, and his mechanics tinkered with FlatFire's engine for 14 years to increase its power. Even though the engine is more than 60 years old, it produces 700 horsepower.

In 2002, FlatFire became the world's fastest flathead-powered car. It reached a top speed of 302 miles (486 kilometers) per hour over a 5-mile (8-kilometer) course. At that speed, anyone watching would just see a blur.

Don Vesco built the Turbinator with his brother.

TURBINATOR

In the mid-1990s, brothers Rick and Don Vesco wanted to do something no one had ever tried before. They put the turbine engine from a military helicopter into a car. The brothers spent a lot of time and effort to make that powerful turbine work like a car engine.

Their work paid off. In October 2001, the Vescos took the Turbinator to the Bonneville Salt Flats in Utah. The car traveled faster than anyone could have guessed. In fact, it sped down the flats faster than any wheel-driven car had ever gone. At 458 miles (737 kilometers) per hour, the Turbinator beat the old record by 55 miles (89 kilometers) per hour.

HORSEPOWER:	3,750
ENGINE:	T55-L-11A SA gas turbine
POWERED BY:	Jet A fuel
TOP SPEED:	458 miles (737 kilometers) per hour
BUILDERS:	Rick and Don Vesco

THRUST SSC

The Thrust SSC broke the sound barrier on October 15, 1997.

HORSEPOWER:	110,000
ENGINE:	Two Rolls-Royce Spey jet engines
TOP SPEED:	763 miles (1,228 kilometers) per hour
OWNER:	Richard Noble
DRIVER:	Andy Green

Two jet engines give the Thrust SSC its amazing speed and power.

The Thrust SSC is in a class by itself. No other car on earth stands a chance against it.

The SSC is basically a jet plane without wings. In fact, its two engines were taken from a jet plane. They produce an amazing 110,000 horsepower.

In 1997, jet pilot Andy Green rocketed across the Nevada desert in the SSC. Green and his team wanted to travel faster than the speed of sound. Sound travels at about 761 miles (1,225 kilometers) per hour. Green just made it. He drove the Thrust SSC across the Nevada desert at 763 miles (1,228 kilometers) per hour. Green became the first person to go faster than sound on land.

The World's FASTEST CARS

10

MURCIÉLAGO

9

ENZO FERRARI

MCLAREN F1

8

7

KOENIGSEGG CCR

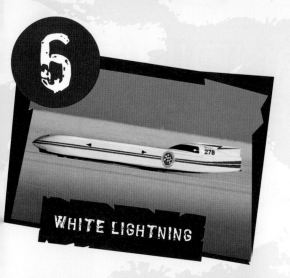

6

WHITE LIGHTNING

BUGATTI VEYRON

5

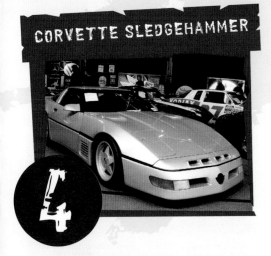

CORVETTE SLEDGEHAMMER

4

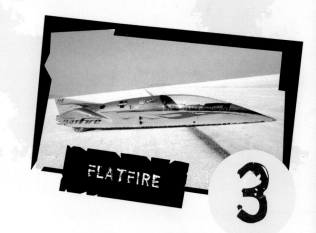

FLATFIRE

3

2

TURBINATOR

THRUST SSC

1

UNDERSTANDING FAST CARS

People always test the limits of what is possible. That includes getting from one place to another in the shortest amount of time.

In a few years, this list of super-fast cars likely will be replaced by a group of faster, more aerodynamic vehicles. People might even laugh at the fact that we thought these vehicles were fast. But car fans will continue to be amazed by the hard work that went into making the cars speed down the road.

One day, cars might move from racing on the highways to streaking through the sky. Even then, the need for speed will inspire people to push the limits. Remember that the next time you buckle yourself in for a drive.

Andy Green drives the experimental MG EX255.

GLOSSARY

aerodynamic (air-oh-dye-NAM-mik)—designed to reduce air resistance

chassis (CHASS-ee)—the frame on which the body of a vehicle is built

cylinder (SIL-uhn-dur)—a hollow area inside an engine in which fuel burns to create power

horsepower (HORSS-pou-ur)—a unit for measuring the power of an engine

production car (pruh-DUHK-shuhn CAR)—a car made in a factory and meant to be driven on streets and highways

turbine (TUR-buhn)—an engine powered by water, steam, or gas that moves through the blades of a fanlike device and makes it turn

turbocharger (TUR-boh-charj-uhr)—a device that forces air into an engine so it can burn gas more quickly and have more power

Read More

Cook, Nick. *The World's Fastest Cars.* Built for Speed. Mankato, Minn.: Capstone Press, 2001.

Dubowski, Mark. *Superfast Cars.* Ultimate Speed. New York: Bearport, 2006.

Graham, Ian. *Sports Cars.* Designed for Success. Chicago: Heinemann, 2003.

Simon, Seymour. *Cool Cars.* SeeMore Readers. New York: Seastar Books, 2003.

Internet Sites

FactHound offers a safe, fun way to find Internet sites related to this book. All of the sites on FactHound have been researched by our staff.

Here's how:

1. Visit *www.facthound.com*
2. Type in this special code **073685455X** for age-appropriate sites. Or enter a search word related to this book for a more general search.
3. Click on the **Fetch It** button.

FactHound will fetch the best sites for you!

INDEX